5-11

Military Heroes

CLARA
BARTON

CLARA BARTON

CIVIL WAR HERO & AMERICAN RED CROSS FOUNDER

by Susan E. Hamen

Content Consultant:
Aeleah Soine, PhD
Visiting Assistant Professor of History, Macalester College

ABDO
Publishing Company

CREDITS

Published by ABDO Publishing Company, 8000 West 78th Street, Edina, Minnesota 55439. Copyright © 2010 by Abdo Consulting Group, Inc. International copyrights reserved in all countries. No part of this book may be reproduced in any form without written permission from the publisher. The Essential Library™ is a trademark and logo of ABDO Publishing Company.

Printed in the United States of America,
North Mankato, Minnesota
102009
012010

 PRINTED ON RECYCLED PAPER

Editor: Chrös McDougall
Copy Editor: Paula Lewis
Interior Design and Production: Emily Love
Cover Design: Emily Love

Library of Congress Cataloging-in-Publication Data
Hamen, Susan E.
  Clara Barton : Civil War hero & American Red Cross founder / Susan E. Hamen.
      p. cm. — (Military heroes)
  Includes bibliographical references and index.
  ISBN 978-1-60453-960-8
  1. Barton, Clara, 1821-1912—Juvenile literature. 2. American Red Cross—Biography—Juvenile literature. 3. Nurses—United States—Biography—Juvenile literature. 4. Women—United States—Biography—Juvenile literature. I. Title.

  HV569.B3H34 2010
  361.7'634092—dc22
  [B]
                                      2009032363

TABLE OF CONTENTS

The Confederate army attacked Fort Sumter, South Carolina, on April 12, 1861.

BAPTISM BY FIRE

In April 1861, the United States was a country divided. The Southern states valued rural agriculture, while the Northern states had many growing industrial cities. The North and South also disagreed about the practice of slavery.

Nineteen Northern states were free states in which slavery was prohibited. But the South consisted of 15 slave states. In an attempt to preserve their plantation-based economy and way of life, which depended upon slavery, 11 of the Southern states seceded from the United States. They declared themselves the Confederate States of America. This plunged the United States into a four-year war that would tear the nation apart and cost the lives of approximately 620,000 soldiers—more American lives lost than in any other war.

The American Civil War (1861–1865) began on April 12, 1861, when the Confederate army fired on Fort Sumter, a U.S. military post situated on an island in the harbor of Charleston, South Carolina. The following day, Major Robert Anderson surrendered to Confederate General Pierre G. T. Beauregard.

A Call for Nurses

Up until the time of the American Civil War, wives, mothers, and servants did most nursing at home. Outside private homes, nurses were typically male. Throughout the course of the war, however, this changed.

The need for nurses increased during the war. Advertisements were placed in newspapers asking for male nurses to come to the aid of the soldiers. However, able-bodied men were expected to fight as soldiers. This opened the door for women to take positions as nurses. By the end of the war, nurses were predominately female.

Two famous authors, Louisa May Alcott and Walt Whitman, both volunteered as nurses during the war. Both later wrote about their experiences.

Supplies for the Troops

As the nation braced itself for war, one woman in Washington DC had been making preparations to aid the soldiers. Forty-year-old Clara Barton, a former schoolteacher from Massachusetts, had stockpiles of medical supplies, food, and clothing in her home and in warehouses. She had been collecting donations for months in preparation for the battles that were sure to come.

Carnage at Bull Run

On August 30, 1862, Union troops from the

North fell to the Confederate army at the Second Battle of Bull Run at Manassas, Virginia. Word reached the capital that 10,000 men were dead and thousands more were wounded. Along with two assistants, Ada Morrell and Lydia F. Haskell, Barton packed three boxcars with supplies she had collected. The next day, the three women traveled by train to Fairfax Station, Virginia, where Barton planned to distribute supplies and tend the wounded.

A Horrific Sight

When Barton and her female companions stepped off the train at Fairfax Station, the sight before them was horrific and grim. Stretcher after stretcher was carried into the surgeons' makeshift operating rooms. Barton noted "their knives and uprolled sleeves and blood-smeared aprons, and by their sides ghastly heaps of cut off legs and arms."[1]

From the moment the women arrived, they were hard at work caring for 3,000 wounded Union soldiers. Field surgeons worked on screaming men— amputated arms and legs were left in piles. Barton and her helpers began bandaging wounds, tying slings, and trying to comfort the men. The women applied compresses and tightened tourniquets around bleeding stumps.

Despite her carefully planned medical and food supplies, Barton found herself sorely lacking cooking utensils. With only two water buckets, one kettle, and a handful of tin cups, plates, and dishes, the

*The union army, left, fell to the confederate army
at the Second Battle of Bull Run in 1862.*

task of preparing food for 3,000 people seemed
insurmountable. But Barton, a levelheaded woman
who was not afraid of hard work, kindled a fire in the
rain and began heating soup and coffee.

The women used the jars and cans that held
jellies, fruits, and preserves as serving dishes to offer
bread and soup or wine to the men. They made sure
all the soldiers received some form of nourishment.

Caring for the Wounded

Night set in as the women continued to feed
and bandage the weak and dying soldiers. Barton

and her assistants wrapped the men in blankets and put donated socks and slippers on their cold, damp feet. When they had used the last of the blankets and quilts, the women tucked hay around the remaining men to help fight off the damp cold.

The women carefully stepped over the bleeding men. They were lying so close together on the ground that navigating among them was nearly impossible. "The slightest misstep brought a torrent of groans from some poor mangled fellow in your path," Barton later recalled.[2]

A Familiar Face

While Barton tended to the men, a young, fair-haired soldier lying on the ground recognized her. Despite being badly wounded with a shattered right arm, Charles Hamilton, a former pupil of Barton's, threw his left arm around Barton and cried. After being comforted by his former teacher, the boy reminded Barton, "I am Charley Hamilton, who used to carry your satchel home from school!"[3] Barton later commented on the sad result of war in her diary, "My faithful pupil, poor Charley. That mangled right arm will never carry a satchel again."[4]

Around 3:00 a.m., a surgeon approached Barton and explained that a young man who was dying from a gunshot wound had been crying for hours for his sister Mary. The surgeon explained that the boy could not survive much longer. He begged Barton to go to the young man and pretend to be his sister to offer him some comfort in his final moments. Barton followed the surgeon to where the boy lay on the ground. She knelt down and cradled him in her lap. In the morning, Barton found that the young man had miraculously survived through the night. The grateful lad, who was now aware that his gracious comforter was not his sister, asked Barton for help. He convinced her to make sure he was put onto the train bound for Washington DC, so that when he died, his body would be returned to his mother. Barton saw to his last request. She later learned the young man, named Hugh Johnson, had survived long enough to see his mother and his sister Mary one final time before he passed away.

"Spirit of Desperation"

As the day progressed, wounded soldiers were loaded onto the train. Confederate soldiers still lurked in the nearby woods. All day, Barton and the Union army expected another attack. Under this lingering threat, Barton and 50 helpers fed the soldiers, dug graves, and buried the dead. Fires were built and soup was distributed. More wagonloads of wounded men arrived. A thunderstorm blew in, and despite the rain, the women continued to work.

Barton's assistants were thoroughly worn-out. Her food supplies were nearly depleted. After the train left, transporting another shipment of wounded soldiers, Barton lay in the corner of a wet tent amid boxes and baskets and tried to sleep. She had barely eaten in more than two days and had virtually no rest. But two hours later, she was awakened by the sound of more wagons arriving with the wounded. She arose, wrung out her wet skirts, and got back to work.

By 3:00 that afternoon, Confederate forces were approaching. But Barton refused to leave any of the men behind. "Our work must be accomplished, and

Serving All Soldiers

Barton was adamant that every wounded soldier should be fed. She later described Monday morning at Manassas: "Train after train of cars were rushing on for the wounded and hundreds of wagons were bringing them in from the field still held by the enemy, where some poor sufferers had lain three days with no visible means of sustenance. If immediately placed upon the trains and not detained, at least twenty-four hours must elapse before they could be in the hospital and properly nourished. They were already famishing, weak and sinking from loss of blood and they could ill afford a further fast of twenty-four hours."[5]

no wounded men . . . once given into our hands must be left, and with the spirit of desperation we struggled on," Barton wrote.[6]

FLEEING FAIRFAX

By 5:00 p.m., all the wounded men had been transported. An officer raced up to Barton and told her she must leave right away if she wanted to make it safely out of Fairfax. She boarded the train immediately. Barton had left Washington on Saturday, and she returned on Wednesday morning. She had just two hours of sleep from Saturday morning until Tuesday night. Upon arriving home, she slept for 24 hours.

The things Barton had seen at Fairfax would change her life, and her future actions would alter the destiny of countless American Civil War soldiers. Although fame was not her goal, Barton would become one of the most celebrated humanitarians of her time. Her relief efforts would become legendary and gain the attention of kings and queens. Clara Barton had much work ahead of her.

Helping Out

Women in Washington DC and neighboring towns were vital in Barton's mission. Barton relied on these women for donations that included items such as food, clothing, medicines, liquor, blankets, bandages, pencils, and paper. Women helped raise funds to buy supplies. They also helped collect, make, organize, and send them to support the soldiers.

Clara Barton treated thousands of men on the Civil War battlefields.

*Clara Barton's birthplace in North Oxford, Massachusetts,
is now a museum with memorabilia of her life.*

EARLY LIFE

On December 25, 1821, Clarissa Harlowe
Barton was born to Stephen Barton
and Sarah Stone Barton in a small, white cottage
in North Oxford, Massachusetts. The family called
her Clara, and she had four older siblings—Dorothy

(Dolly), age 17; Stephen, age 15; David, age 13; and Sally, who was ten.

Clara's "Soldier Father"

Stephen was a successful farmer, horse breeder, and local politician. A well-respected member of their community, he often moderated town meetings. He regularly donated money to help the poor and homeless and used his own funds to establish a house for the poor. Earlier in his life, he had been a soldier and fought in battles against American Indians alongside future U.S. President William Henry Harrison. He had been present when Tecumseh, the great Shawnee leader, was slain during the War of 1812.

Sitting on her father's lap, Clara would listen to countless stories about war. Stephen would paint vivid tales of battles, describing every detail to the young girl. From her father, whom she called her "soldier father," Clara learned a great deal about military strategy and tactics. She also credited her father with giving her an undying sense of patriotic pride. She wrote, "I early learned that next to Heaven, our highest duty was to love and serve our country and honor and support its laws."[1]

LESSONS FROM A STERN MOTHER

Clara's mother was a hardworking woman who taught Clara household skills such as sewing, cooking, and gardening. Clara also learned to make soap, weave cloth, can fruits, and milk cows. Sarah Barton was a plain, commonsense housewife who had little time or patience for frivolous things. She saw no need for Clara to have toys or dolls. Clara helped her sisters with household chores and learned not to complain or fuss.

A HOUSEHOLD OF TEACHERS

Clara's parents were not the only ones at home who passed on valuable knowledge. Her older brothers and sisters all contributed to her education. When Clara was born, her oldest sister, Dolly, was already a schoolteacher and would later help care for her little sister.

Stephen, her oldest brother, also became a teacher when Clara was young. But he took over their father's textile mill, along with brother David, after a few years. Stephen was

"I had no playmates, but in effect six fathers and mothers. They were a family of school-teachers. All took charge of me, all educated me, each according to personal taste. My two sisters were scholars and artistic, and strove in that direction. My brothers were strong, ruddy, daring young men, full of life and business."[2]

—*Clara Barton*

a noted mathematician and patiently taught Clara arithmetic on her small slate.

David was not as interested in scholarly pursuits. His interests revolved more around animals and the outdoors. He taught Clara how to drive a nail with a hammer, throw like a boy, and tie a square knot. He taught her about horses and how to ride. David was a bit of a daredevil, and under his instruction, Clara learned to ride bareback on the family's Thoroughbreds. Clara was five years old when David, then 18, sat her atop a horse. He instructed her to hang on tight to its mane, and they rode together across the countryside. Her riding skills would save her later on the occasions when she was forced to flee from approaching Confederate troops.

Though ten years older, Sally was the sibling closest in age to Clara. Sally also taught school for a short while. She was responsible for introducing Clara to literature and poetry. Together, the sisters would

Parents Knew Best

From each of her parents, Clara learned invaluable skills that she would put to great use later in life. Thanks to her father's lessons, military rank and order was second nature by the time she reached the front lines of the American Civil War. She never confused colonels, lieutenants, or majors. And she was well versed in military etiquette. Just as important, she was able to prioritize cooking and bandaging duties, focusing on the work that needed to be done—just as her mother had taught her.

read English poetry and the writings of Sir Walter Scott, the Scottish novelist and poet. Clara described Sally as "lovely as a summer morning."[3]

A SHY, TIMID GIRL

Clara was a shy girl who seldom spoke up or complained. She had very few friends her own age. Because she was so much younger than the rest of the family, she often felt intimidated during family discussions. When she did attempt to add to the conversation, the others were often amused by her childish comments. This caused Clara to become self-conscious, timid, and withdrawn.

Later, when Clara went to school, she left the classroom in tears after her fellow students laughed when she mispronounced the name of Ptolemy, a Greek mathematician. Although Clara struggled with her timidity, she was comfortable in some areas of life. She was confident when saddling her horse and loved to ride carefree across her father's land.

A PROPER EDUCATION

Clara entered school before she turned four and could already read and spell three-syllable words. Each year, school met for two terms, each three

Clara Barton's field desk sits behind a large spinning wheel at the Clara Barton Birthplace Museum.

months long. On Clara's first day of school, Colonel Richard C. Stone, the schoolteacher, asked her to spell *cat* and *dog*. She informed him that she could spell *artichoke*. Colonel Stone then placed her in an advanced reading class.

In May, school reopened for the next term. Clara found herself the only Barton at school, which was scary for a shy young girl. But her teacher, Susan Torrey, kindly reassured her. When school resumed the following term, her teachers had taken different teaching jobs. Clara's sisters Dolly and Sally became the schoolteachers during the summer, and Stephen taught the winter term.

Off to Boarding School

In 1829, when she turned eight, Clara's parents sent her to a boarding school run by her former teacher, Colonel Stone. Her parents believed the separation from home would do her good and help her overcome her shyness. But Clara was miserable. She soon stopped eating and grew thin and pale. Colonel Stone and the local doctor decided it was best to send her home.

By this time, Clara's family

An Eloquent Writer

At the age of 13, Clara began pasting poems and verses that caught her fancy into a scrapbook. She had a talent for writing poetic verse. She started writing diaries as a girl. Through the years, she recorded her thoughts and reactions to the ups and downs of her life on the battlefield, in the company of European royalty, and during the formation the American Red Cross. Her diaries and letters are full of examples of her eloquent writing. She also kept mementos and scrapbooks from her many journeys.

During bouts of depression, Barton wrote very little in her diaries. However, her letters to family and friends serve as a record of her mood and thoughts.

After her death, Barton's family passed her diaries, letters, medals, and mementos to the Library of Congress in Washington DC. Many of these items are now displayed at her final home, Glen Echo, Maryland, which is now a National Historic Site run by the National Park Service.

had purchased and moved to a 300-acre (121-ha) farm. Joining them on the farm were the Learneds, the widow of her father's nephew and her four children. On the farm, Clara enjoyed the freedom of exploring the wooded hills and playing with the animals. She enjoyed the company of her cousins and running around the grounds.

NURSING BROTHER DAVID

When Clara was 11, her brother David fell from the top of a barn he was helping to build. Initially, he seemed to be all right. However, he quickly began to suffer from headaches and fevers that kept him bedridden for two years. Clara quit school during that time to stay home and take care of him.

In those days, doctors often prescribed leeching as a remedy for persistent fevers. They believed that using leeches to draw blood would cure the patient by removing excess blood from the body. Clara dutifully applied the "loathsome crawling

Extended Families

Typically, households today consist of nuclear families—parents and their children. But it was common for nineteenth-century households to include extended family members, such as grandparents, aunts, uncles, and cousins. The Bartons later lived with extended family on a farm.

Many families also took in boarders. These strangers would pay a small fee for a bedroom and meals. It was not uncommon for a family acquaintance to stay as a guest in a home during an extended visit. Typically, only children of the wealthy had their own bedrooms.

leeches" to her brother, but his condition only worsened.[4]

Finally, a young doctor suggested a steam bath cure. Although the steam bath was not responsible for David's cure, it did put an end to the leeching. That allowed David to make a full recovery in three weeks. ⌒

*A photo of young Clara and other personal items are
on display at her birthplace.*

Chapter 3

Built in 1839, the New Jersey schoolhouse in which Barton taught still stands.

MISS BARTON, THE SCHOOLTEACHER

*I*n 1834, when Clara's brother David was declared healthy once again, 13-year-old Clara turned back to her studies. Tutor Lucian Burleigh instructed her in history, language, English literature, and composition. The following year,

Clara enrolled in school again. Jonathan Dana, an intelligent, able teacher, gave her lessons in advanced philosophy, chemistry, and Latin. All of Clara's teachers marveled at how diligent she was in her schoolwork and how she craved to learn about any subjects she could.

Clara the Mill Girl

Clara insisted on keeping busy when school was not in session. She asked to work at her brothers' mill, the Satinet Mill of North Oxford, weaving cloth. At first, her parents objected. But her brother Stephen agreed that it would help her stay busy. He built a little platform for his small sister to stand on.

In 1835, Clara learned to operate a flying shuttle on a large loom. She was happy to be productive and proud that she had accomplished the skill of weaving at the loom. Her employment lasted a short two weeks,

A Destination Wedding

In September of 1840, Barton's love for adventure and travel grew when she had the opportunity to travel to Maine. Her brother David asked her to join him on a steamer bound for Portland, Maine, and then on to Kennebec County, Maine, where he would marry Julia Porter. This was the first time Barton had traveled by ocean. She was awestruck by her adventure, which included a night in a fancy hotel in Boston. She was even more surprised when she was asked to be a bridesmaid.

however, because the mill burned to the ground. Unable to continue weaving, Clara next turned her energy to following the family tradition of teaching.

In Front of the Classroom

Dressed in a new green dress fashioned to make her look older, Clara stood in front of her first class in a little schoolhouse near her sister Sally's home. It was May 1839, and Clara was 18 years old. She was nervous as she stood in front of her 40 students, who ranged in age from toddlers to

Early U.S. Schools

Today, public schools are available to all children in the United States. Laws require children to attend school until the age of 16 in many states and 17 or 18 in others. Every child is entitled to an education. But this has not always been the case.

In the eighteenth and nineteenth centuries, the majority of schools were one-room schoolhouses that taught children as young as three or four as well as teenagers. The Protestant or Congregational churches ran most of the schools.

Usually, schools were open only a few months at a time. This allowed children to help their families with farmwork. Not all adults believed children needed a school education. Children as young as three were often responsible for simple tasks around the home. Other children, some as young as five, worked full-time at mills or factories to help support their families.

By 1776, only about half of the 14 states had instituted plans for public education. By the 1800s, reformers argued that public schools, called common schools, would bring together children from various immigrant backgrounds and help create good citizens.

In 1852, Massachusetts became the first state to pass school-attendance laws. By 1918, all states required that children receive at least an elementary-school education.

boys just a few years younger than she was. She was unsure of how to speak to her class, so she pulled out the Bible and turned to the New Testament. Each student took a turn reading a verse from the Sermon on the Mount.

At recess, the older, rowdier boys were surprised when their tiny teacher joined them in a game and demonstrated her athletic ability. "My four lads soon perceived that I was no stranger to their sports or their tricks," she explained.[1] She immediately gained their respect and admiration, unlike the previous teacher, whom the boys had driven from the school.

DISCIPLINING AT MILLWARD

Miss Barton proved to be a successful teacher. By the end of her first term, her small school was awarded high ratings in North Oxford for discipline. The following

Romance

When Barton was in her twenties, she was torn by matters of the heart. Her many journals and letters mention nothing about a romantic relationship, but it seems she did have a suitor or two. One gentleman she met while teaching in North Oxford moved to California during the gold rush of 1849 and made a fortune. He wrote to Barton, asking her to move to California and marry him. Although she refused, he sent her $10,000, which she saved for years. She did not spend it until she had exhausted her own money buying supplies for her soldiers.

summer, she was offered a position at Millward, a school in the neighboring village of Charlton. Millward was known for its boisterous, unruly students.

Millward was just far enough away that Barton had to move out of the family home when she accepted the new teaching post. She quickly discovered the students at her new school were a much rougher group than her first students. Earning two dollars a week, she was now in charge of 50 youngsters who were in need of some stern discipline.

At first Barton tried to win over the students with smiles and kindness, but that failed. The older, rowdier boys continued to disrupt the classroom. One morning, the ringleader of the troublemakers came to class late. Upon his arrival, he mocked her and upset the classroom. Barton asked him to step to the front of the class. She took a riding whip

Future Soldiers

Barton taught scores of children, many of whom would serve during the American Civil War. She wrote, "Scattered over the world, some near, some far, I have been their confidante, standing at their nuptials if possible, lent my name to their babies, followed their fortunes to war's gory field, staunched their blood, dressed their wounds, and closed their Northern eyes on the hard-fought fields of the Southland."[2]

from her desk and lashed him. The entire class was shocked. The boy stood up and apologized to Barton and the rest of the class. After that day, she had no more problems with the students of Millward.

Word spread that Miss Barton had a knack for enforcing discipline in her classrooms. She was transferred from one problem school to the next, turning classrooms around. Her students admired and loved their small teacher.

CLARA'S MILL SCHOOL

Clara approached her brothers and asked to start a school for the factory children whose parents worked in the family's mills. Her brothers gave her a small room in their mill, where she taught 70 children. Eventually, Stephen and David built a schoolhouse for her where she instructed 125 pupils. Clara taught at the factory school and also acted as Stephen's bookkeeper.

THE FIRST PUBLIC SCHOOL IN NEW JERSEY

In 1852, Barton grew restless. She enrolled in Clinton Liberal Institute, a school in New York State. While there, she discovered there was no public school in the town of Bordentown, New

Jersey. She believed she could be successful in setting one up. But others told her she would surely fail. Barton offered, "Give me three months and I will teach free."[3]

Barton became the first person to open a public school in New Jersey. Her school grew from 6 students to 600 one year later. But she was demoted to being only a schoolmistress, and a man was put in charge of running the school. Barton was devastated that the school she had created and run for two years had been handed over to someone else, simply because she was a woman. That spring, when an ailment of her vocal cords made it difficult to talk, she submitted her resignation. She would never teach again.

The Importance of Red

From a young age, Barton's favorite color was red. "It is my color," she often said.[4] Throughout her life, she often added a red ribbon or bow to her dress, and in later years, she could be seen wearing red bonnets, shawls, and capes. As an adult, Barton was instrumental in creating the American Red Cross. Even the Barton family coat of arms contained red, the color of sacrifice.

Barton left teaching for good after being demoted to schoolmistress of her school in New Jersey.

Washington DC in 1850, four years before Barton arrived

LIFE IN WASHINGTON DC

Barton left New Jersey for Washington DC in February 1854. She hoped the warmer climate there might help her voice. She would spend most of the next 60 years in the United States' capital city.

Through Colonel Alexander DeWitt, a distant cousin and a congressman from her home district, she was able to find work in the Patent Office as a clerk under Judge Charles Mason, the commissioner of patents. Although clerks at the Patent Office were usually men, Mason recognized Barton's superb handwriting and her diligent work. She was the first woman to work full-time in the Patent Office.

False Accusations and Sexism

A patent gives an inventor the right to exclusively produce and sell his or her creation. At the time, some of the male clerks were guilty of leaking patent secrets and selling them, much to the damage of the inventors who held the patents. Mason soon saw that Barton was honest, hardworking, and trustworthy. He appointed her to a position at a confidential desk, overseeing secret documents. She was given the same salary the men were earning—$1,400 per year—which was quite a large sum for a woman at that time.

Perfect Penmanship

While working for her brother as a bookkeeper, Barton learned to write in the "copperplate" fashion. This neat, elegant style of cursive handwriting was used by bookkeepers, lawyers, and business-men. Thomas Jefferson mastered this style of writing. His perfect cop-perplate handwriting can be seen on the Declaration of Independence.

Soon, the men in the Patent Office became jealous of Barton. They harassed her and falsely accused her of misconduct. Several of these men were those who sold secrets. Mason put an end to the accusations and fired the men who had brought the false allegations against Barton.

In her free time, Barton enjoyed life in Washington. She spent time strolling or picnicking outdoors and enjoying the flowers and blossoming trees. She viewed life in Washington as very exciting, and she enjoyed watching

Job Opportunities for Women of the 1850s

While working for the U.S. Patent Office, Barton made a lot of money for a woman of her time. Unmarried women of her day usually had some sort of job, often working in someone else's home or doing piecework for outside profit. Most women who worked outside their home took jobs as schoolteachers, maids, or servants. But these positions paid very poorly.

The Industrial Revolution, which began in the early nineteenth century, opened up opportunities for women to work at mills and, later, factories. But these "mill girls," as they were called, worked in dangerous and miserable conditions. They received approximately $2 a week for their work in the loud, hot mills. At her highest salary, Barton was bringing in nearly $27 a week.

Women were not allowed into many colleges. Society thought it improper and absurd for women to try to become doctors, lawyers, and engineers. Women were believed to be too weak-minded and lacking in physical strength to work in such fields.

Some female-dominated professions were emerging, however. More and more women began to take jobs in nursing, teaching, and social work, especially after the Civil War.

the lively, fashionable people walking the streets of the growing city. She also attended political speeches at the Capitol building and became interested in politics.

In the fall of 1855, President Franklin Pierce and Secretary of the Interior Robert McClelland made it their goal to rid all government offices of women employees. Mason stood up for Barton and praised her work. McClelland said she could continue with her employment as long as she could perform her duties outside of the office.

DIVISIONS AND ALLIES

In May 1856, Barton had the opportunity to see Massachusetts Senator Charles Sumner speak before the Senate about the injustice of slavery. Barton was spellbound as she listened to Sumner argue against expanding slavery into the U.S. territories. The next day, Sumner was attacked and severely beaten by a congressman from the South.

The attack on Sumner caused a great stir among both Northerners

A Pioneer for Women

While working in the Patent Office, Barton endured cruel treatment by her male colleagues. Some would spit tobacco juice at her, and others would make rude comments or blow smoke in her face. She ignored the terrible treatment and carried on with her work. Barton broke down a long-standing barrier for women and intended to continue pioneering new opportunities for other women.

*Barton was inspired by the words
of Massachusetts Senator Charles Sumner.*

and Southerners. It was evident to many Americans that the division over the subject of slavery was pushing the country closer to war.

In 1857, when James Buchanan became president, neither Alexander DeWitt nor Mason was able to advocate for Barton as government employees were dismissed on the grounds of political differences of opinion. Anyone belonging to the

Republican Party, which at the time had progressive ideas that were unpopular in the South, was at risk. Barton lost her job in the Patent Office. She returned to North Oxford for two years, studying French and art, but longed to return to Washington.

Two years after she had been let go, Republican Abraham Lincoln was elected president. Now, Republicans at the Patent Office were able to offer Barton a job. They asked her to return to help organize the documents and paperwork that had been messed up during her absence. Her salary would be lower than before, and she could not earn more than $900 per year. Despite the decrease in pay, Barton happily returned to Washington.

As Barton's political views grew stronger, she realized that befriending people in powerful positions in Washington would benefit her in the future. She no longer had DeWitt and Mason to secure her position at the Patent Office. It was time to make new friends within the new Republican delegation in Washington.

Barton sought out Senator Henry Wilson in March 1861, and the two

Equal Pay

Barton once refused a teaching position because the same position would pay a man more money. "I may sometimes be willing to teach for nothing, but if paid at all, I shall never do a man's work for less than a man's pay.'"[1]

became friends. Wilson would stand behind her and champion her causes throughout the American Civil War and beyond. They met regularly to talk and discuss politics in Washington. Trusted by Lincoln, Wilson was later appointed chairman of the Committee on Military Affairs. Barton's new friend would become a very powerful ally during the war and after.

A New President

On March 4, 1861, Barton was present as Abraham Lincoln, a Republican from Illinois, delivered his inaugural address. The new president's speech addressed the issues of slavery and secession. Lincoln wished to avoid a civil war and explained that his intention was not to interfere with slavery in the states in which it was already legal. He went on to warn, however, that secession by any states would not be tolerated.

Barton was invited to the inauguration ball, although she could not attend due to a severe cold. She was at the center of America's political pulse. Soon, she would have a front-row view of the turmoil the country would wage on the battlefields of the Civil War. ⌒

Abraham Lincoln was elected president of the United States of America in 1860 and took office in 1861.

Union soldiers arrive in Baltimore's Monument Square in April 1861.

WAR

When the South fired on Fort Sumter on April 12, 1861, President Abraham Lincoln declared war and asked for 75,000 volunteer soldiers to defend Washington DC from rebels. Militiamen and neighborhood groups of volunteer soldiers answered the call. Four days after the attack on Fort Sumter, the Sixth Massachusetts Regiment of the Union army boarded a train bound for Baltimore, Maryland, on their way to the capital. Approximately 40 of the young men had once been students of Clara Barton. They arrived in Baltimore on April 19.

Riots in Baltimore

The majority of the citizens of Baltimore supported secession. They were angered by the Union troops passing through their city on the way to Washington. As the soldiers walked from one train platform to another, which was nearly a half mile (0.8 km) away, they were attacked by a mob of 10,000 infuriated Baltimore residents. Three soldiers in the Sixth Massachusetts Regiment were killed and another 30 were wounded. The American Civil War had claimed its first casualties.

News of the attack reached Washington by telegraph. Crowds of

Reflections on War

Barton described the first few days of tending to the injured soldiers of the Sixth Massachusetts Regiment in a letter to a friend: "So far as our poor efforts can reach, they shall never lack a kindly hand or a sister's sympathy if they come. In my opinion this city will be attacked within the next sixty days. If it must be, let it come; and when there is no longer a soldier's arm to raise the Stars and Stripes above our Capitol, may God give strength to mine."[1]

people made their way to the B&O Railroad depot to await the arrival of the wounded soldiers. Barton and her sister Sally, who was visiting, made their way to the station. Barton had made up her mind to help the soldiers in any way she could.

Transportation and Technology

The first ambulances used during the war consisted of two-wheeled carts pulled by a horse or mule. However, these jostled the patients. By 1862, the Union and Confederate armies used covered wagon ambulances. Men assigned to each ambulance carried the injured on stretchers and loaded them into the wagons. This was the first time ambulance units were used by American troops.

The Union army utilized the new railroad systems to transport the injured men to Washington DC for long-term care. At first, the men were laid upon straw strewn on the floor of boxcars. But before the war ended, hospital train cars were designed with beds strung three tiers high.

Many new technologies were used during the war. Telegraph operators traveled with the army. Telegraph poles and wire were set up in order to quickly send news of the battles back to Washington. Newspaper reporters moved with the troops and sent stories home for publication.

Hot air balloons were also used during the war so officers could view far-off battlefields and monitor the progress of battles. Photography, which was becoming popular at the time, captured images of soldiers and battlefields. The war was photographed so much that many say it was better documented than any other war until World War II.

TENT CITY

Washington was unprepared for the arrival of so many soldiers. Haphazard quarters were set up for the men, and some were housed in the Capitol building. Tents sprung up all around the city. As Barton moved amid the ragged, injured soldiers in the Senate chamber, she recognized some as former students. They were relieved to see a familiar face. Most had "*nothing* but their heavy woolen clothes—not a cotton shirt and many of them not even a pocket handkerchief" after their luggage had been seized in Baltimore.[2]

Barton was driven to action. She went home and gathered supplies for the regiment. Old sheets were torn up to be used for handkerchiefs and towels. She filled baskets and boxes with food and other supplies. Barton had found her purpose. Her patriotic heart burned to serve her country, and she could do that by providing food and comfort to the troops.

News Spreads

Through word of mouth, news spread about Barton's relief efforts. Soon, she was collecting goods from churches, families, sewing circles, and anyone else who would donate. She placed an ad in the *Worcester Spy* asking for aid. She also wrote to friends in Massachusetts and New Jersey, asking them to send any goods they could spare.

Her rented rooms began to overflow with clothing, bandages, jellies, liquors, preserves, medicines, and all manner of supplies. Barton was

Union soldiers await medical attention after a battle in July 1862.

forced to rent a warehouse near Seventh Street and
Pennsylvania Avenue. Within six months, she would
fill three warehouses.

In the weeks following the Baltimore attack,
Barton's sister Sally helped her treat the soldiers who
were camped on the hills around Washington. They
tended to the men's injuries, delivered supplies,
wrote letters home for them, and read them the
newspaper. They passed out sewing kits, paper,
and by special request of Colonel Stephen Miller,
tobacco.

A Father's Blessing

In late 1861, Barton was called home as her father lay dying. Sitting at his bedside, she wrote to Governor John A. Andrew of Massachusetts. She had met the governor through an old friend, Colonel DeWitt, and asked for help to get to the front lines to assist the troops. She wrote, "I would [be eager] to go and administer comfort to our brave men, who peril life and limb."[3]

"When the [train] cars whistled up to the station, the first person on the platform was Miss Barton to again supply us with bandages, brandy, wine, prepared soup, jellies, meals, and every article that could be thought of."[5]

—*Doctor James Dunn, at Fairfax Station, speaking of the Second Battle of Bull Run*

Barton's father approved of her work on behalf of the troops and gave her his blessing to go to the battlefields. The man who had taught her everything she knew about military tactics and soldiering assured her, "Soldiers, however rough, always respect a woman who deserves it."[4] The following day, at the age of 88, Captain Stephen Barton died.

Determined to gain permission to aid the injured soldiers at the front, Clara immediately returned to Washington DC. As she worked to stock her warehouses, she heard of the Union losses of 6,000 soldiers at the Battle of Fair Oaks. More than 8,000 were wounded during the Seven Days' Battles.

CLARA'S PATRIOT BLOOD

With the "patriot blood of [her] father . . . warm in [her] veins," Barton decided to quit her job as a patent clerk and go into "direct service of the sick and wounded troops wherever found."[6] Although she would face strong opposition, she would make it her mission to help the wounded men on the battlefield.

TO THE FRONT

Army officials repeatedly refused to grant Barton permission to serve on the battlefield, so she did not expect anything different when she met with Colonel Daniel H. Rucker, assistant quartermaster general in charge of transportation. She said to him, "I have no fear of the battlefield. I have large stores but no way to reach the troops." Rucker was so impressed by her earnest plea, he immediately issued her a permit and an order for six wagons to haul her supplies and men to help load them. He also gave her written requests that asked other high-ranking army officials to allow Barton to pass through lines on her way to the front. Major Rucker handed her the paperwork she had been desperately seeking, telling her, "Here is your permit to go to the front, and God bless you."[7]

The Union lost 6,000 soldiers at the Battle of Fair Oaks on May 31, 1862.

*Barton earned her nickname "Angel of the Battlefield"
after the Battle of Cedar Mountain.*

ANGEL OF THE
BATTLEFIELD

With all the proper permits and passes,
Clara Barton was ready to go to the
battlefield. Wearing a long, dark skirt, a plaid jacket,
and a kerchief, Barton sat in a wagon among bales
and boxes of supplies. She arrived at Culpeper,

Virginia, two days after the Battle of
Cedar Mountain, which had taken
place on August 9, 1862. As her
wagon pulled up to the hospital at
midnight, Brigade Surgeon James
L. Dunn was astounded to discover
that Barton had brought bandages,
dressings, and supplies. The hospital
was out of the much-needed items.
Dunn praised Barton saying, "I
thought that night if heaven ever sent
out a holy angel, she must be one,
her assistance was so timely."[1] It was Dunn who later
gave her the nickname "Angel of the Battlefield."

"And so Began My Work"

Barton set to work nursing the injured men who
lined the bare floors of the homes in Culpeper.
Some were missing arms and legs. She gave them
bread soaked in wine and cooked applesauce and
soup. She handed out clean shirts and tried to help
the doctors whenever she could. About Culpeper,
Barton wrote, "When our armies fought on Cedar
Mountain, I broke the shackles and went to the field.
And so began my work."[2]

By this time, other organizations had been founded to help wounded soldiers. The U.S. Sanitary Commission, formed in New York by concerned civilians, provided supplies and medicine to the sick and wounded from the North. Dorothea Dix was appointed the Union's superintendent of the Army Nursing Corps, which tended to wounded soldiers. Although Barton respected these other organizations of mercy, she preferred to work alone and be in charge of her own supplies.

Barton's assistance at Culpeper was still far removed from the gunpowder and cannon blasts of the battlefields.

The Sanitary Commission

The Sanitary Commission was a relief organization that was founded by New York civilians in 1861. Church congregations, ladies' aid groups, and concerned citizens came together to form the commission, which collected supplies and organized their distribution for Union soldiers.

Women from as far away as Chicago sent knitted and sewn articles, fruit preserves, and other items to the Sanitary Commission. The commission delivered food, clothing, medicine, and supplies to the sick and wounded. While reviewing camps and hospitals, commission inspectors stressed the importance of sanitation and ventilation to avoid dangerous outbreaks of disease.

Although they did not work directly together, Barton wrote that she and the Sanitary Commission were on good terms. Barton frequently relied on the Sanitary Commission for goods and transportation. She was aware of the organization's efficiency and complete stock of supplies as early as the Second Battle of Bull Run.

However, she was not prepared for the chaos and horrors she witnessed. Simple necessities such as clean bandages and fresh water were lacking. Supplies were days late in coming, and the surgeons used one table to operate on man after man.

Immediately upon returning to Washington DC, Barton started resupplying her warehouses. She had used three warehouses' worth of supplies for one battle. On August 30, 1862, she learned of the large number of wounded soldiers at the Second Battle of Bull Run and made hasty preparations to leave.

HARPERS FERRY

In the days following her exhausting efforts at the Second Battle of Bull Run, Barton continued to prepare for the next time she could be of assistance. Her chance came just days later. Early on the morning of September 13, 1862, an army messenger handed her a piece of paper bearing the words, "Harpers Ferry—not a moment to be lost."[3] Ironically, after making Barton fight so hard to gain permission to be on the battlefield, army officers were now giving her advance notice of anticipated battles. They also provided her with four wagons, supplies, mules, and men to drive the wagons

Union soldiers stormed the engine house at Harpers Ferry, West Virginia.

approximately 80 miles (128 km) to Harpers Ferry, West Virginia.

However, the army felt the safest place for Barton was at the end of a very long line of soldiers and wagons carrying ammunition, food, and clothing. Barton knew it was vital to get medical supplies to the injured men. The group spent the day traveling through the hills of Maryland, passing wounded soldiers and countless bodies of those who had fought Thomas "Stonewall" Jackson's men and surrendered at South Mountain. She and one of her men, Cornelius "Cornie" Welles, climbed over bodies trying to assist any survivors. Very few were still alive.

As the army made camp and bedded down for the night, she convinced her drivers to arise at 1:00 a.m. to harness the wagons and move to the front of the line. By morning, they had caught up to the head of the line approximately ten miles (16 km) down the road. They were now positioned behind the cannon and in front of the ammunition wagons.

A Lucky Break

When Barton ran out of food at the farmhouse at Antietam, she discovered that three of the twelve cases of wine she brought had been packed using cornmeal instead of sawdust. "If it had been gold dust it would have seemed poor by comparison," Barton explained.[4] Clara used the cornmeal to make gruel for the men.

ANTIETAM

On their way to Harpers Ferry, the wagon train came upon the valley of Antietam near Sharpsburg, Maryland. General Robert E. Lee and about 52,000 Confederate troops had made their way into Maryland and were camped near Antietam Creek. Across the creek, General George B. McClellan and his army of some 70,000 Union soldiers anxiously awaited daybreak. The Union troops had suffered a series of defeats at the hands of the Confederate generals and were eager for victory.

On her way to assist at Harpers Ferry, Barton had come across what would be the bloodiest battle of the American Civil War.

As the first rays of dawn broke over the eastern skies of the Blue Ridge Mountains, the bugle sounded and fighting broke out. The Confederates opened fire. Major General Joseph "Fighting Joe" Hooker of the Union army led his unit south, straight into the men of Lieutenant General Stonewall Jackson. As the troops clashed, Barton readied her men and wagons to move with the cavalry and artillery, following where the fighting would be the most intense.

Corn Leaves for Bandages

After lumbering eight miles (12.8 km) across fields, Barton stopped her wagons at a farmhouse next to a tall cornfield. Dunn had set up a medical station in the house for those too injured to travel to the field hospital. As Barton pulled up, she saw four tables on the front porch. Laid upon each table was a soldier awaiting surgery. The surgeons, lacking supplies, were forced to use green corn leaves for bandages. The doctors were overjoyed to see Barton and her supplies.

Barton wasted no time. Her men unloaded the wagons and she began preparing food. Fighting had spread into the cornfield, and Barton instructed 12 men to help locate wounded soldiers among the rows of stalks. She helped administer chloroform to anesthetize men prior to surgery and passed out wine to dull the pain of those with the worst wounds.

Selfless Bravery

Amid gunfire, constant smoke, and the booming cannons, Barton helped arrange the wounded men in the barn and corncribs. One aid estimated that approximately 1,500 men were tended at the farmhouse. With no concern for her own safety or comfort, Barton mercifully cared for the soldiers she referred to as "my boys."

As Barton and her crew worked into the night, one surgeon gave up hope, complaining there was not a

Clara the Surgeon

One of the young wounded soldiers at Antietam convinced Barton to extract a bullet from his cheek. She refused at first, but the young man insisted that the surgeon should not be bothered when he had far more serious wounds to tend to. Using a pocketknife, she cut into his face as another soldier held his head. She then cleaned and bandaged the wound. Barton had performed her first field surgery.

single candle to light his work. Barton went to her wagon and returned with four boxes of lanterns. Once again, she had come to the rescue with her supplies and planning.

Nearly 23,000 American lives were lost at Antietam before the Confederate army retreated. Despite the nurses' efforts, most of the soldiers they treated died. Dispirited and exhausted after working nonstop, Barton and her men turned their wagons toward Washington to begin their 80-mile (128.7-km) journey home. She arrived in Washington with a fever, still covered in gunpowder.

Clara Barton tended a wounded man in a hospital.

Confederate General Robert E. Lee led the troops at the Battle of Fredericksburg.

CIVIL WAR HEROINE

In December 1862, Union General Ambrose Burnside and the 120,000 men of the Army of the Potomac camped near Falmouth, Virginia. Across the Rappahannock River near Fredericksburg, General Robert E. Lee and 78,000

Confederate troops waited. Meanwhile, Clara Barton had set up a hospital at Lacy House, a large mansion that faced the river. There, she waited for the next day's battle and expected the worst.

On December 12, Union engineers attempted to construct a pontoon bridge so troops could cross the river. Men were repeatedly shot down by Confederate sharpshooters, who were hiding in cellars in homes on the other side. As Barton watched soldiers pick up where fallen comrades left off, she noted, "And ever here and there a man drops in the waiting ranks, silently as a snow flake."[1] Even Lacy House became a target to some of the bullets whizzing across the river. Finally, the Union men made it across.

The Battle of Fredericksburg was bloody and chaotic. Soldiers lay bleeding on the ground, their clothing and bodies freezing to the icy earth. In the thick of combat, Barton was given a piece of bloodied paper sent by Brigade Surgeon J. Clarence Cutter. It instructed her, "Come to me. Your place is here."[2] Despite exploding artillery and showers of bullets, Barton made her

"In my feeble estimation, General McClellan, with all his laurels [honors], sinks into insignificance beside the true heroine of the age, the angel of the battlefield."[3]

—Dr. James L. Dunn, surgeon at the Battle of Antietam, 1862

Union Casualties

Approximately 360,000 Union soldiers died during the war. Of these:
- 110,000 died in combat or from wounds from combat
- 224,586 died of disease, including diarrhea and dysentery, typhoid, and malaria

way across the swaying, makeshift bridge to administer to the wounded men in Fredericksburg.

While cannonballs and musket fire ripped through the city, Barton made her way to the wounded and dying soldiers. She comforted them and did her best to bandage them. Sadly, she found familiar faces among the wounded.

Hundreds of injured men were taken back across the river to Lacy House. There, Barton spent two weeks tending to the men who lay on bare floors, which were slippery with blood. Patients were crammed into every space of Lacy House, including under tables and on pantry shelves. The North suffered a terrible defeat at Fredericksburg. Of the 18,000 who died there, almost 13,000 were Union soldiers.

Three months later, when Barton returned to Washington DC, she was summoned to Lincoln Hospital. As she entered Ward 17, 70 patients saluted her. Those who were able to stand did so while others sat up in bed. Each of the men had been under her care at Lacy House.

The Campaign against Sumter

In April 1863, the Union army began the siege of Charleston, South Carolina, with the goal of taking Fort Sumter, Fort Wagner, and Fort Gregg. All of these were Confederate strongholds. Barton traveled to Hilton Head, South Carolina, where her brother David was stationed as a captain in the Union army. She arrived just as the Union troops were about to attack.

Retaking Fort Sumter would be difficult, so the Union army turned its attention to attacking Fort Wagner in early July. Barton was ready with all the supplies she could muster, tending to the wounded in a tent on the hot sands of Morris Island. She nursed white soldiers and African-American soldiers alike. She was credited with saving the lives of two generals and a colonel. After being shot, Colonel Elwell awoke to see Barton caring for him. He described the experience, "Clara Barton was there, an angel of mercy doing all in mortal power to soothe my pain."[4]

The siege at Fort Wagner lasted eight months. The rigors of war were

Overcrowding

Lacy House was so crowded with wounded men that many had to be placed outside on the muddy, icy yard on blankets. Barton warmed bricks in the fireplace and tucked them around the men shivering in the cold December air. When someone in the house died, another soldier was moved inside.

taking their toll on Barton. She had always kept a detailed journal, but her entries became shorter and less frequent. The hot climate, sand, and sea of South Carolina affected her eyes, feet, nose, and lungs. She grew thin and sick, but she would not slow down. In January 1864, Barton headed back to Washington DC to secure more supplies for the coming battles.

HORRORS AT FREDERICKSBURG

In May of 1864, Barton went to Fredericksburg to care for the wounded soldiers

Dorothea Dix

Dorothea Dix was another humanitarian who worked hard to earn sympathy and compassion for her causes. Born in 1802 in Maine, Dix opened a school for girls in Massachusetts and taught for a number of years.

In 1841, Dix volunteered to teach a Sunday school for women in a Massachusetts prison. She was appalled at the conditions and disturbed to see how the mentally ill inmates were treated. She began a two-year tour examining similar institutions and reported her lengthy findings to the Massachusetts legislature.

In 1861, she became the superintendent of Union army nurses during the Civil War. Although she struggled as a leader and was often at odds with the doctors, Dix and her nurses offered needed care to suffering, wounded soldiers. She was known for her passion for patient advocacy.

Dix spent 40 years lobbying state legislatures and Congress, helping to establish 32 state hospitals for mentally ill patients. She also organized, staffed, and helped train the personnel at her hospitals.

Dix and Clara Barton never formally worked together and did not always agree with each other's methods. However, they were part of a common voluntary movement of female nurses who were active during the American Civil War.

from the Battle of Spotsylvania Court House and the Battle of Cold Harbor. There, she was appalled by what she found. Seven thousand wounded soldiers had been left in Fredericksburg. No homes or businesses would take in the bleeding, dying men. Officers did not enforce their right to seize the town's supplies. Wagons filled with wounded amputees had been left stuck in deep mud. Men begged for food and water but were given none. The railroad and canals leading out of town had been barricaded by the townspeople, prohibiting the transfer of the wounded back to Washington DC.

Horrified, and with the power to do very little, Barton made her way back to Washington and notified her old friend Senator Henry Wilson. He took her complaint straight to the Department of War. By 2:00 a.m. the following day, officials arrived in Fredericksburg. The city's homes were opened to the wounded soldiers and the railroad and canal were unblocked.

NURSING A BROTHER

In September 1864, Barton's brother Stephen fled his home in

Keeping Record

During the battle at Fredericksburg, doctors were so busy helping the wounded that they did not have time to keep medical records. Barton, however, wrote down the names of the men who died and where they had been buried.

North Carolina, where he had moved before the war. The South was losing, and many Southerners became refugees, leaving their homes and lands as battles raged around them.

Stephen was viewed as a traitor for selling cotton to the North and using the money to purchase drugs and medicines that he, in turn, sold in the South. He was imprisoned, and his personal property was seized. When news reached Barton, she enlisted the help of a Union general to free him. When she saw Stephen, she was surprised to find a thin, feeble man who walked with a cane. Her once healthy and robust brother was now in need of bed rest and a nurse. For six weeks, Barton devoted her time and attention to helping care for her brother in Washington DC.

In March 1865, Stephen Barton died. Barton returned home to Massachusetts with his body for burial. A month later, on April 9, General Lee surrendered to Union General Ulysses S. Grant at Appomattox Court House, Virginia. The American Civil War had come to an end. —

Confederate General Robert E. Lee surrendered to Union General
Ulysses S. Grant in 1865, ending the American Civil War.

A sign from one of Barton's homes in Washington DC

MORE WORK TO BE DONE

With the war over, Clara Barton had no job. While nursing her brother Stephen in February and March, she had written to President Lincoln and requested permission to aid in locating missing soldiers. The president was pleased that Barton, a woman who had served these men throughout the course of the war, would help locate the more than 80,000 missing soldiers. He provided her with a letter that read:

To the Friends of Missing Persons:

Miss Clara Barton has kindly offered to search for the missing prisoners of war. Please address her at Annapolis, giving her name, regiment, and company of any missing prisoner.

Signed

A. Lincoln[1]

Barton arrived in Annapolis, Maryland, on March 11, 1865. She set up her office and began searching for missing men. In Annapolis, thousands of prisoners of war were returned to the North from Southern prisons. But few, if any, records were kept to track these men. Thousands were simply sent home, leaving no clue as to who had been released and who remained imprisoned. Barton immediately went to work organizing and creating records.

Unknown Soldiers

When the American Civil War ended in 1865, the quartermaster of the federal army reported 359,528 deaths among the Union troops during the course of the war. Of those, only 315,555 had graves. Only 172,400 of those graves were identified. A total of 143,155 men lay in unidentified graves. A total of 43,973 men had no listed burial site. Many of these men were never buried.

John Wilkes Booth shot Abraham Lincoln on April 14, 1865.

On April 14, 1865, John Wilkes Booth shot President Lincoln in Ford's Theater in Washington DC. The president died the next morning. Barton would pursue her cause without further support from Lincoln.

By May, Barton was receiving more than 100 letters a day from families searching for loved ones. She began publishing lists of the missing in local newspapers and posting the lists in post offices. She relied on information from veterans who might recognize the names of fellow soldiers.

The Office of Correspondence with Friends of
the Missing Men of the United States Army operated
from a tent. Barton did her best to respond to the
thousands of letters she received. From 1865 to
1869, Barton received 63,182 letters and responded
to each. The office identified 22,000 men. She
received meager funding from the government and
relied heavily on her own savings to fund her office.

ANDERSONVILLE

In June 1865, Barton received
a letter from Dorence Atwater, a
20-year-old man who had been
held at Andersonville Prison in
the South. "I brought a copy of the
Death Register from the Rebel Prison
at Andersonville, Georgia," he
wrote.[2] While in prison, it had been
Atwater's responsibility to record the
name, regiment, and cause of death
of each prisoner who had died. He
had made a secret copy of the death
register, which he smuggled out of
the prison when he was transferred.

Travel Companions

Barton and Dorence
Atwater continued to
work together after building the Andersonville
National Cemetery. Atwa-
ter traveled with Barton
during her lectures and
acted as her assistant. One
night, traveling through
Illinois, the train jumped
the tracks and Barton's
coach car landed upside
down. She was pinned to
the ceiling under a stove
with hot coals strewn
across her. Atwater helped
her out of the car and the
two proceeded to the next
town.

Atwater described the inhumane conditions at Andersonville, which resulted in the deaths of as many as 100 prisoners a day. Little to no fresh water, crammed quarters, no shelter, and severe beatings resulted in the deaths of nearly 13,000 of the 32,000 prisoners. The dead had been buried in mass trench graves with numbered sticks serving as grave markers.

Barton wanted to publish the list and travel to Andersonville to rebury the dead in properly marked graves. Secretary of War Edwin Stanton summoned Barton to his office. He praised her efforts

Women's Rights Movement

Barton gained recognition as a public speaker. Suffragists Susan B. Anthony, Lucy Stone, and Elizabeth Cady Stanton asked her to join them in their goal of gaining the right for women to vote. The women, who formed the National American Woman Suffrage Association, saw that Barton's speaking engagements drew large crowds of men as well as women. They believed that with her support, more men would listen to their cause.

Anthony invited Barton to join them at the American Equal Rights Association meeting in New York in 1869. But Barton's health was poor. She did not fully agree with the other women's methods, but she did become lifelong friends with Anthony.

From 1848 into the 1900s, Anthony and Stanton fought to win the right of women's suffrage. They traveled around the country, speaking publicly to rally women—and men—to support women's rights. They endured sarcasm, abuse, and, at times, were arrested and fined. In 1920, due in part to the efforts of Anthony and Stanton, the Nineteenth Amendment to the United States Constitution granted women the right to vote.

and assured her she had the backing of the U.S. Army.

Barton traveled to Andersonville with a crew of 40 men. They reburied 12,800 bodies of Union soldiers and 400 bodies of Confederate soldiers and performed Christian burial rites. When they were finished, Barton raised the Stars and Stripes above the Andersonville National Cemetery.

THE LECTURE CIRCUIT

Following her work at Andersonville, Barton hoped to continue her search for missing soldiers. But with her money nearly gone, she needed a form of income. She had spent some $12,000 of her own money during the war. To raise money, she charged a fee to deliver lectures about her experiences with the war. Soon, she had 300 lectures scheduled across the country.

Her lecture circuit was very successful. She was able to earn between $75 and $100 for each lecture—the same that male lecturers

A Young Namesake

During a lecture at a YMCA hall, a familiar-looking man approached Barton. She asked him if they knew each other. He explained how she had nursed him at the Second Battle of Bull Run, the Battle of Fredericksburg, and in Petersburg. Barton remembered the face. She looked down at his little girl and asked him if she was his daughter. "Yes," he replied. "She is almost three years old and we call her Clara Barton."[3]

received—plus expenses in some cases. Some months her income was as much as $1,000. Congress had voted to reimburse Barton the $15,000 she had spent locating missing soldiers. That, coupled with the money she earned from her lectures, made her financially secure. The office she had established to locate missing soldiers could carry on.

She traveled across the country for two years on trains, sleeping in hotel rooms and speaking to large audiences. She spoke passionately about the soldiers she had aided and the battles she had witnessed. People were spellbound as she recounted her experiences on the battlefields. Barton became a household name. People flocked to her lectures to listen to the Angel of the Battlefield.

After two years of lecturing, Barton was exhausted from constant travel. And one night in 1868, prior to a lecture, she found her voice had given out. Her doctor prescribed a trip to Europe for several months of relaxation and escape.

Within a few months, Barton was in better health. Together with her sister Sally, Barton boarded the *Caledonia* in August 1869, bound for England. At the age of 47, Barton would find her next rigorous calling across the ocean. ⌐

Clara Barton in 1865

Jean Henri Dunant was the founder of the International Red Cross and the 1901 Nobel Peace Prize winner.

Barton and the Red Cross

Clara Barton and her sister Sally arrived in Glasgow, Scotland, in the fall of 1869. Clara then traveled on alone, and eventually made her way to Geneva, Switzerland. There, she was visited by a group of Swiss dignitaries. The group, which included Doctor Louis Appia, was active in establishing the International Red Cross. They had heard of her valiant war efforts and came to discuss an important treaty with her.

The Geneva Convention

Swiss banker Jean Henri Dunant helped found the International Red Cross in 1863 in response to the horrible conditions he encountered during the Battle of Solferino in 1859. Five years later, 22 countries had signed the Treaty at Geneva, also known as the Geneva Convention. This treaty set up rules of conduct during war. One of its stipulations was that the sick and wounded, as well as all doctors, nurses, and ambulances, could not be attacked. It further stated that medical personnel attending the wounded or sick must not take sides in the conflict. Any person or vehicle displaying a red cross or red crescent—two symbols of medical aid workers—was to be protected.

Appia told Barton the United States had been asked to sign the Geneva Convention twice, but it had declined both times. Barton was shocked to learn her country had not signed the treaty. She wrote, "As I counted up its roll of 22 nations, not a civilized people in the world but ourselves missing, and saw Greece, Spain, and Turkey there, I began to fear that in the eyes of the rest of mankind we could not be far from barbarians. . . . I grew more and more ashamed."[1]

THE FRANCO-PRUSSIAN WAR

Barton would soon have the opportunity to see the International Red Cross in action. On July 15, 1870, Napoleon III of France declared war against King Wilhelm I of Prussia, an area that is now part of Germany.

When the war broke out, Barton was in Bern, Switzerland, hoping to recuperate at the therapeutic baths. Wilhelm I's daughter, Grand Duchess Louise of Baden, called on her one day. The grand duchess praised Barton for her work during the American Civil War and asked that she come to Strasbourg, France, to organize relief following the fighting there.

Appia and the International Red Cross also asked Barton to offer her leadership and knowledge at the front lines. Barton explained that she had still not recovered and that her doctor had advised complete rest for three years.

RETURNING TO THE FRONT

Yet, as Barton thought of the suffering and great need of those at the front, she was moved to action. Barton traveled to the International Red Cross headquarters in Basel, Switzerland, where she helped organize the large shipments of supplies that were arriving. After one week, she was

Red Cross and Red Crescent

The Red Cross and Red Crescent is an international organization that provides relief to those injured or suffering in major crises throughout the world. Its work is based on seven fundamental principles: humanity, impartiality, neutrality, independence, voluntary service, universality, and unity.

Jean Henri Dunant established the International Red Cross and Red Crescent Movement in 1859 after he witnessed the Battle of Solferino in Italy. During the battle, 40,000 Austrians and Frenchmen were killed. Dunant organized emergency aid to the wounded. His experiences prompted him to propose the formation of an international neutral relief organization.

In 1863, he founded the International Committee for the Relief of the Wounded, which would later be called the International Committee of the Red Cross. The introduction of the Geneva Convention followed the next year and was signed by 12 European nations. Within three years, all the major European powers had signed the treaty. The Red Crescent was officially adopted in 1906 and represents Muslim countries, although both the Red Cross and the Red Crescent function as one organization.

Today, there are 186 National Red Cross and Red Crescent Societies around the world. The International Red Cross and Red Crescent Movement has been awarded the Nobel Peace Prize three times.

anxious to get to the front lines. Barton left with Antoinette Margot, a young Swiss woman who served as a French and German translator. The two traveled to Mulhouse, France.

On the way to Mulhouse, Barton and Margot passed large groups of refugees fleeing to Switzerland. Entire families and their livestock lined the roads. Cows and oxen pulled carts loaded with household possessions. Some people carried what they could in their arms. The wealthier refugees rode in carriages and wagons loaded with their things. The frightened French warned them, "The Prussians are coming! Turn back, turn back!"[2] But Barton and Margot continued on.

Upon reaching Mulhouse, they found their services were not needed. The two women pressed on to Strasbourg. They traveled through rain and cold; transportation was difficult. When they finally arrived in Strasbourg, they found they were needed most in Haguenau, the center of a deadly struggle.

Losing Sight

In the early months of 1872, Barton became temporary blinded and had to keep her eyes bandaged. Her eyes had been damaged by cannon smoke from her years on battlefields. However, she refused to remain idle and learned to write letters without the use of her eyesight.

When Barton arrived in Brumath, where the wounded from Haguenau were taken, she was not allowed anywhere near the soldiers.

ASSISTING THE VICTIMS OF WAR

Barton's health improved as she began helping refugees. She traveled across the war-torn countries of France and Germany. She provided medical treatment, collected and distributed food and clothing, and offered comfort to the starving and freezing citizens of the warring countries. A young woman named Anna Zimmermann joined in helping Barton and Margot, and the three worked to help where they could.

Unlike her service during the American Civil War, Barton's relief work with the Red Cross in Europe was with civilian victims of war, not with wounded soldiers. She helped women, children, and the elderly. She worked in cities that had been left in rubble with very few homes, businesses, or factories still standing.

Sewing Workrooms

During her relief work in Strasbourg, Barton realized that handing out food and clothing on a daily basis would do very little for the long-term benefit of the victims of Strasbourg. What the people needed was a recovery plan that included employment. Barton set up workrooms where women of Strasbourg sewed 30,000 garments. The seamstresses earned wages for their work. This gave them money for food and supplies and answered the need for clothing for thousands of poverty-stricken victims.

Townspeople had no shelter, no food, and little hope of rebuilding. Barton not only helped feed and clothe these victims, but she helped set up recovery plans to empower them to help themselves and return their lives to normal.

Rewarded by the German Royalty

Barton's acts of mercy with the Red Cross in Europe were noticed and rewarded. Grand Duchess Louise presented Barton with a large amethyst brooch shaped like a pansy, which became one of Barton's most cherished possessions. Louise also presented Barton with her first Red Cross pin. From the Emperor and Empress of Germany, she received the Iron Cross of Merit.

Exhausted and ill again, Barton traveled to Italy and then on to London with Margot in search of rest and recuperation. But the cold, wet, and dark climate of London made her even more ill. Under the fog of London, she longed for a bright, sunny day. Her throat and chest gave her trouble. She was weak, homesick, and depressed.

In October 1873, at the age of 51, Barton decided to return to Washington DC. She had one goal in mind: establish the Red Cross in America.

*Clara Barton, with a red cross on her chest, worked
with the German army.*

Later in life, Clara Barton yearned to establish the Red Cross in America.

THE RED CROSS
COMES TO AMERICA

pon returning to Washington DC in 1873, Barton learned that her sister Sally was gravely ill. She rushed home to Massachusetts, but Sally had already died. Clara was crushed. She sank into a deep depression and became sick with stomach ailments, fevers, and headaches. She spent months at her family's homes in Worcester and North Oxford. She became so ill that she could barely leave her bed most days.

Barton finally began to recover at a sanitarium in Dansville, New York. Physician James Caleb Jackson prescribed fresh air, sunshine, healthy foods, therapeutic baths, and rest to treat his patients. By the winter of 1877, Barton felt well enough to move into a rented house in Dansville.

Barton had not forgotten her goal of establishing the Red Cross in America. She wrote to her friend Louis Appia of the International Red Cross and explained her four-year illness. She said she was ready to move forward with her plans. "Like the old war horse that has rested long in quiet pastures," she wrote, "I recognize the bugle-note that calls me to my place, and, though I may not do what I once could, I am come to offer what I may."[1]

Appia replied to Barton's letter, urging her to head the organization in America. Barton began meeting with government officials, asking them to see the benefit of an American Red Cross. She wrote and circulated brochures, gave talks to small groups, and also met with President Rutherford

B. Hayes. He referred Barton on to Secretary of State W. M. Evarts. Instead of meeting with Barton, Evarts had his assistant, Frederick W. Seward, handle the matter. Seward's father, William, had been responsible for originally refusing to sign the Geneva Convention. The younger Seward was just as cold to the idea of an American Red Cross.

In late 1880, James A. Garfield was elected president. Barton was hopeful that she now would make headway with her cause. She and Garfield knew each other from their battlefield days, when Garfield was a major general. Upon meeting Garfield after his inauguration, she discussed the Red Cross with him. He asked her to present her information to the new secretary of state, James G. Blaine. Fortunately, Blaine showed an immediate interest.

News began spreading of Barton's efforts to establish the Red Cross in America. On May 12, 1881, she organized a meeting of individuals who were interested in the Red Cross. Barton described to them the organization's purpose and services. By the end of the night, those 22 people in attendance agreed to become charter members of the American Red Cross. On May 21, at another meeting, the American Association of the Red Cross was officially formed. Later in June, its officers were elected. Barton continued to publicize and speak about the organization, but the assassination of President Garfield in September 1881 threatened the future of Barton's American Red Cross.

Chester A. Arthur became president upon the death of Garfield. During his presidency, Congress ratified the Geneva Convention in 1882. The United States became a member country of the International Red Cross. Clara Barton became president of the American Red Cross.

Recognition

When Barton assisted South Carolina's Sea Islands following a hurricane, several African Americans approached her. They explained that she had nursed their wounds at Hilton Head during the Civil War. They showed her their scars and praised her efforts. One elderly African-American woman had walked 30 miles (48 km) to see her. The woman had cooked for Barton while they were at Hilton Head.

Some had feared that the commitment of the Red Cross to neutrality would endanger U.S. security during times of war. The U.S. government feared spying and sabotage if the Red Cross was given frontline access. Thus, the American Red Cross was founded to provide humanitarian relief during times of natural disasters and other crises, as opposed to the relief provided on the battlefields by the Red Cross in Europe.

Dansville, New York, became the first local branch of the American Red Cross. A few weeks later, with the help of Susan B. Anthony, a famous suffragist fighting for women's right to vote, a local branch opened in Rochester, New York. Syracuse and Onondaga County, New York, followed soon after.

The first time the American Red Cross offered help was in 1881 during a forest fire in Michigan. The organization provided food, clothing, and medical supplies, followed by lumber, tools, and household goods to the victims of the fire.

When the Ohio River flooded in February

A Flood in Johnstown

In 1889, Barton and the Red Cross rushed to bring relief to the victims of the Johnstown, Pennsylvania, flood. Nearly 34,000 people were killed in what was one of the deadliest disasters in U.S. history.

Barton and her 50 workers arrived to a town in chaos. Despite skepticism by the Pennsylvania militia, Barton set up her office in a tent and went to work. She remained in Johnstown for five months, enduring the rain and terrible conditions. Shipments of supplies began to arrive, and homes, hotels, and businesses were rebuilt. Approximately 20,000 people received assistance from the Red Cross, all under the careful guidance of Barton.

The grateful citizens of Johnstown presented her with a new "medal" to add to her collection—a gold pendant encrusted with diamonds and sapphires. The *Johnstown Daily Tribune* sang the praises of Barton, writing, "Hunt the dictionaries of all languages through and you will not find the signs to express our appreciation of her and her work. Try to describe the sunshine, try to describe the starlight. Words fail."[2]

1884, people and livestock were swept away on raging currents. Towns in Ohio and Illinois were completely destroyed. Barton dispersed aid and supplies from a riverboat. By the time she returned to Washington DC, she had traveled 8,000 miles (12,875 km) on the river and handed out $175,000 in money and supplies.

In the fall of 1888, the Red Cross responded to a deadly yellow fever epidemic in Jacksonville, Florida. When Russia fell victim to a famine in 1889 and 1890, Barton arranged for U.S. aid to be sent overseas. The American Red Cross also offered its services to Turkey and Armenia in Europe. In 1898, the Red Cross went to Cuba, where the United States was battling Spain in the Spanish-American War over the liberation of Cuba.

Barton's Red Cross Days Come to an End

Throughout her decades of relief work, Barton usually ran things by herself. Her work during the Spanish-American War had established the Red Cross as a vital organization operating in the United States and abroad. In 1900, she ventured into her last disaster zone when Galveston, Texas, was hit by a hurricane. Barton was 80 years old.

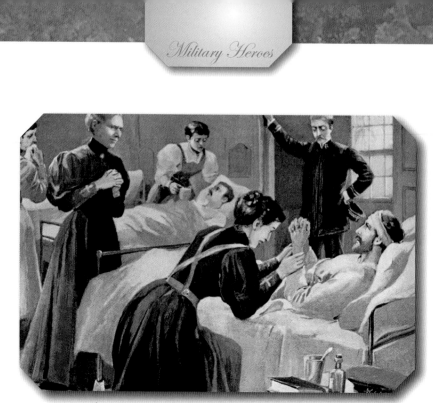

Clara Barton worked with Red Cross nurses in 1898.

That year, the Red Cross set up a board of directors to run the organization. Barton was not happy about having to clear everything through them. She had worked very hard to establish the Red Cross in America, and she was losing control of it.

In the summer of 1902, she attended the Seventh International Red Cross Conference in St. Petersburg, Russia. Lavish reception parties and banquets were held to honor Barton, who had become a hero in the eyes of European royalty. Czar Nicholas II presented her with the Silver Cross of Imperial Russia, the country's highest civilian honor, in recognition of the aid she had provided for the Russian famine victims ten years earlier.

Upon Barton's return to the United States, she learned that Mount Pelée, on the island of Martinique, had erupted on May 8. Approximately 40,000 people were killed. The Red Cross board members felt they did not have the money or resources to help the victims, and so they did nothing. Barton was furious.

Increasingly, Barton and the board of directors began to have very differing views on how to run the organization. Some board members felt it was time for Barton, now more than 80 years old, to resign. Some members also accused Barton of stealing and mismanaging Red Cross funds. In March 1904, a formal complaint was filed against her with the Senate. Among other accusations, it claimed that Barton diverted Russian famine relief money for aid in Texas.

The congressional committee assigned to investigate the allegations found no proof of any wrongdoing on Barton's part. But the ordeal left her shocked and bitter, and she turned in her resignation on May 14, 1904. The *Chicago Inter Ocean* said about her resignation, "Clara Barton cannot resign her place in the world as the one real, true representative of the Red Cross of this country."[3] During the 23 years she was involved with the American Red Cross, she dispersed an estimated $2 million in aid during 18 relief efforts.

FINAL YEARS

Barton retired to her home at Glen Echo, Maryland. She began working on a book entitled *A Story of the Red Cross.* In 1907, she wrote a short book about her youth entitled *The Story of My Childhood.* While she had intended it to be the first in a series of books about her life, she wrote no additional books.

Even well into her eighties, Barton arose early every morning to do the washing, cooking, and cleaning. Most days, she could be seen in her bonnet, walking out to milk her Jersey cow. She often wore a shawl and her glorious medals and pins.

"For more than forty years, I have known dear, beloved Miss Clara Barton. Great affection and great admiration and great gratitude united me with her. Never shall I forget what she had been to us here in the year 1870, helping us in such a wonderful way during the time of war we had to go through then. She was one of those who understood fully the meaning of the Red Cross, and who knew well, how to put in action the great and beautiful though difficult duties the Red Cross involves in itself."[4]

— *Grand Duchess Louise of Baden*

In the winter of 1910, Barton came down with pneumonia. This was followed by a bout of bronchitis. But she pulled through. In July 1911, she visited her childhood home in North Oxford with her nephew Stephen Barton. Christmas brought her ninetieth birthday and another battle with double pneumonia. For several months, Barton teetered between life and death.

In her final days, Barton often dreamed of being back on the battlefield. She wrote, "I dreamed I was back in battle. I waded in blood up to my knees. I saw death as it is on the battle field."[5] Two days later, on Good Friday, April 12, 1912, Clara Barton cried out, "Let me go! Let me go!"[6] After these final words, she died. Her wishes had been for a small funeral service. She was laid to rest in the family plot at the cemetery in North Oxford next to her mother and father.

The mercy and selflessness shown by Barton on the battlefield and in the midst of disasters had never

Noticed in Death

Throughout Barton's life, family members of the men she had helped during the American Civil War thanked her. Even in death, Barton inspired similar gratitude. When her coffin was loaded onto a covered wagon to be transported to North Oxford for burial, the driver threw up his hands. In disbelief, he remarked, "My God, is this the body of Clara Barton? Why, my father was a Confederate soldier and at the battle of Antietam he was wounded in the neck and was bleeding to death when Miss Barton found him on the battlefield and bound up his wounds in time to save his life."[7]

before been seen. She was a woman who dedicated her life to lessening the suffering of strangers. In 1892, the government recognized the work of Civil War nurses, including that of Barton, in the passage of the Army Nurses Pension Act. This law entitled the nurses a government pension for their services on the battlefield.

Barton's work lives on today. The American Red Cross stands ready to assist when natural disasters occur. With 700 local chapters, the Red Cross organizes blood donations and is the nation's largest supplier of blood to hospitals. Chapters also offer classes in first aid, CPR, swimming lessons, and lifeguard training. In recent years, the Red Cross has offered support and counseling to military personnel and their families.

The American Red Cross refers to its founder Clara Barton as a "visionary leader."[8] She was truly one of the world's greatest humanitarians. As her cousin, Reverend William E. Barton said, "It was her heroic soul and her deep human sympathy that made her strong and brave."[9]

Clara Barton, Angel of the Battlefield

TIMELINE

1821	1829	1832–1834
Clarissa "Clara" Barton is born on December 25; she is the fifth child of Stephen and Sarah Barton.	Clara is sent to boarding school.	Clara quits school to stay home and nurse her brother David.

1854	1861	1861
In February, Barton moves to Washington DC and becomes the first woman to work in the U.S. Patent Office.	Barton is present when Abraham Lincoln delivers his inaugural address on March 4.	The Confederate army fires upon Fort Sumter on April 12, starting the American Civil War.

1834

Clara returns to her studies and takes advanced classes in philosophy, chemistry, and Latin.

1839

In May, Barton teaches her first class of 40 children at District School No. 9 in North Oxford.

1852

Barton enrolls in Clinton Liberal Institute in New York. She starts the first public school in New Jersey.

1861

The Union army suffers defeat at the First Battle of Bull Run in Virginia on July 21.

1862

On August 9, Barton delivers medical supplies and food to Union troops at the Battle of Cedar Mountain.

1862

The Second Battle of Bull Run is fought on August 30. Barton nurses the wounded.

TIMELINE

1862	1862	1863
The Battle of Antietam on September 17 is the bloodiest battle of the Civil War.	A battle at Fredericksburg, Virginia, begins on December 12. Barton cares for hundreds of men at Lacy House.	An eight-month siege begins in July to capture Fort Wagner. Barton is stationed in South Carolina.

1873	1881	1881
Barton returns to the United States in October determined to convince the United States to sign the Geneva Convention.	The American Association of the Red Cross meets for the first time on May 21.	The American Red Cross offers assistance for the first time during a Michigan forest fire.

1865

General Lee surrenders to General Grant on April 9. The American Civil War comes to an end.

1865

Barton arrives in Annapolis, Maryland, on March 11. She begins locating missing prisoners of war.

1870

The Franco-Prussian War erupts on July 15. Barton assists the International Red Cross relief efforts.

1902

During the summer, Barton attends the Seventh International Red Cross Conference in St. Petersburg, Russia.

1904

On May 14, Barton turns in her resignation as president of the American Red Cross.

1912

Clara Barton dies at her home in Glen Echo, Maryland, on April 12.

Essential Facts

Date of Birth

December 25, 1821

Place of Birth

North Oxford, Massachusetts

Date of Death

April 12, 1912

Parents

Stephen Barton and Sarah Stone Barton

Education

North Oxford District School; Clinton Liberal Institute, New York

Career Highlights

❖ Barton opened a school for the children of the mill workers at her brothers' mill.

❖ In 1852, Barton opened the first public school in New Jersey.

❖ She moved to Washington DC in February 1854 and became the first female patent clerk.

❖ During the American Civil War, Barton collected supplies for Union soldiers and was a nurse on the front lines.

❖ After establishing the American Red Cross in 1881, Barton served as its first president until her resignation on May 14, 1904.

Societal Contribution

Barton provided relief aid to wounded soldiers during the American Civil War. She collected, transported, and dispensed many warehouses' worth of supplies to Union soldiers; she also nursed and fed them. During the Franco-Prussian War in Europe, Barton worked with the International Red Cross to bring disaster relief to thousands. Throughout her many years with the Red Cross, she assisted people around the world during natural disasters.

Conflicts

After setting up the first public school in New Jersey and successfully running it for two years, Barton was given the title of schoolmistress, and a man was brought in to act as superintendant. Later, Barton lost her job in the Patent Office because of her political views.

Barton fought her way through army ranks to finally obtain permission to serve wounded soldiers on the battlefield. Later, Barton faced opposition from U.S. presidents who did not want to sign the Treaty of Geneva. In 1900, the American Red Cross board of directors began efforts to take over control of the organization. Allegations were brought against Barton, but they were later dismissed by a congressional committee.

Quote

"Like the old war horse that has rested long in quiet pastures, I recognize the bugle-note that calls me to my place, and, though I may not do what I once could, I am come to offer what I may."
—*Clara Barton*

ADDITIONAL RESOURCES

SELECT BIBLIOGRAPHY

Barton, Clara. *The Story of My Childhood*. New York, NY: Baker and Taylor Company, 1907.

Barton, William E. *The Life of Clara: Founder of the American Red Cross. Vol. 1*. Cambridge, MA: Riverside Press, 1922.

Epler, Percy H. *The Life of Clara Barton*. New York, NY: MacMillan Company, 1917.

Oates, Stephen B. *A Woman of Valor: Clara Barton and the Civil War*. New York, NY: Free Press, a Division of Macmillan, Inc., 1994.

Pryor, Elizabeth Brown. *Clara Barton: Professional Angel*. Philadelphia, PA: University of Pennsylvania Press, 1987.

Ross, Ishbel. *Angel of the Battlefield: The Life of Clara Barton*. New York, NY: Harper & Brothers Publishers, 1956.

FURTHER READING

Benge, Geoff, and Janet Benge. *Clara Barton: Courage Under Fire*. Lynnwood, WA: Emerald Books, 2003.

Prokos, Anna, et. al. *Clara Barton: Angel of the Battlefield*. Time for Kids Biographies: New York, NY, Collins Publishers, 2008.

WEB LINKS

To learn more about Clara Barton, visit ABDO Publishing Company online at **www.abdopublishing.com**. Web sites about Clara Barton are featured on our Book Links page. These links are routinely monitored and updated to provide the most current information available.

Places to Visit

Andersonville National Cemetery/Andersonville National Historic Site
496 Cemetery Road, Andersonville, GA 31711
229-924-0343
www.nps.gov/ande
The cemetery is the final resting place for prisoners of war who died at Andersonville Prison. It is one of only two active national cemeteries still burying veterans and their dependents.

Clara Barton Birthplace Museum
66 Clara Barton Road, North Oxford, MA 01537-0356
508-987-2056 ext. 213
www.clarabartonbirthplace.org
Guests can tour Clara Barton's childhood home. The museum offers special programs for school groups.

Clara Barton National Historic Site
5801 Oxford Road, Glen Echo, MD 20812
301-320-1410
www.nps.gov/clba
Clara Barton's house in Glen Echo served as her home in her later years as well as a warehouse for relief supplies. The large home was also the headquarters for the American Red Cross. Tours and educational programs are offered.

Red Cross National Headquarters
430 17th St. NW, Washington, DC 20006
202-303-7066
www.redcross.org/museum/history/visitorinfo.asp
The headquarters building houses art and artifacts acquired by the Red Cross. Guided tours of the national headquarters are free. Because the headquarters is a functioning office, tours are offered only at designated times.

Glossary

abolish
> To destroy or end.

amethyst brooch
> A bluish-purple piece of jewelry that is attached to clothes by a hinged pin and catch.

anesthetize
> To use medicine to cause a person to become unconscious.

artillery
> Large, powerful weapons, or the soldiers who operate them.

cavalry
> A group of soldiers mounted on horseback.

chloroform
> A liquid chemical used to induce unconsciousness.

corncrib
> A building for storing and drying corn.

cornmeal
> A powder, or flour, that is ground from corn.

dignitary
> Somebody who holds a high-ranking position or honor.

epidemic
> A fast and widespread outbreak of a disease.

famine
> A severe lack of food.

Geneva Convention
> A treaty that created a standard for humane treatment for those injured during war.

humanitarian
> A person who is dedicated to improving the lives of others.

inauguration
> The formal ceremony at the beginning of a term in political office.

loom
> A tool for weaving threads or yarns into cloth.

philanthropy
> A desire to improve the welfare of humankind.

piecework
> When somebody is paid a certain amount for each unit produced.

pontoon
> A portable float used to construct a temporary bridge.

ratified
> Approved.

sanitarium
> A place for rest and regaining health or strength.

secede
> To withdraw from a group or organization.

suffrage
> The right to vote.

textile mill
> A factory that manufactures cloth or fabric.

tourniquet
> A first-aid device used to stop bleeding by compressing blood vessels.

SOURCE NOTES

Chapter 1. Baptism by Fire

1. Elizabeth Brown Pryor. *Clara Barton: Professional Angel.* Philadelphia, PA: University of Pennsylvania Press, 1987. 93.

2. Percy H. Epler. *The Life of Clara Barton.* New York, NY: MacMillan Company, 1917. 38.

3. Ibid. 39.

4. Ishbel Ross. *Angel of the Battlefield: The Life of Clara Barton.* New York, NY: Harper & Brothers Publishers, 1956. 37.

5. Percy H. Epler. *The Life of Clara Barton.* New York, NY: MacMillan Company, 1917. 42.

6. Ishbel Ross. *Angel of the Battlefield: The Life of Clara Barton.* New York, NY: Harper & Brothers Publishers, 1956. 40.

Chapter 2. Early Life

1. Ishbel Ross. *Angel of the Battlefield: The Life of Clara Barton.* New York, NY: Harper & Brothers Publishers, 1956. 4.

2. William E. Barton. *The Life of Clara: Founder of the American Red Cross. Vol. 1.* Cambridge, MA: Riverside Press, 1922. 22.

3. Elizabeth Brown Pryor. *Clara Barton: Professional Angel.* Philadelphia, PA: University of Pennsylvania Press, 1987. 9.

4. Ibid. 16.

Chapter 3. Miss Barton, the Schoolteacher

1. Elizabeth Brown Pryor. *Clara Barton: Professional Angel.* Philadelphia, PA: University of Pennsylvania Press, 1987. 21.

2. Ishbel Ross. *Angel of the Battlefield: The Life of Clara Barton.* New York, NY: Harper & Brothers Publishers, 1956. 15.

3. Percy H. Epler. *The Life of Clara Barton.* New York, NY: MacMillan Company, 1917. 20.

4. Ishbel Ross. *Angel of the Battlefield: The Life of Clara Barton.* New York, NY: Harper & Brothers Publishers, 1956. 5.

Chapter 4. Life in Washington DC

1. Elizabeth Brown Pryor. *Clara Barton: Professional Angel.* Philadelphia, PA: University of Pennsylvania Press, 1987. 23.

Chapter 5. War

1. William E. Barton. *The Life of Clara: Founder of the American Red Cross.*
Vol. 1. Cambridge, MA: Riverside Press, 1922. 110.
2. Elizabeth Brown Pryor. *Clara Barton: Professional Angel.* Philadelphia,
PA: University of Pennsylvania Press, 1987. 78.
3. Ishbel Ross. *Angel of the Battlefield: The Life of Clara Barton.* New York,
NY: Harper & Brothers Publishers, 1956. 32.
4. Ibid.
5. Elizabeth Brown Pryor. *Clara Barton: Professional Angel.* Philadelphia,
PA: University of Pennsylvania Press, 1987. 93.
6. Percy H. Epler. *The Life of Clara Barton.* New York: MacMillan
Company, 1917. 32.
7. Ishbel Ross. *Angel of the Battlefield: The Life of Clara Barton.* New York,
NY: Harper & Brothers Publishers, 1956. 33.

Chapter 6. Angel of the Battlefield

1. Ishbel Ross. *Angel of the Battlefield: The Life of Clara Barton.* New York,
NY: Harper & Brothers Publishers, 1956. 35.
2. Ibid. 34.
3. Elizabeth Brown Pryor. *Clara Barton: Professional Angel.* Philadelphia,
PA: University of Pennsylvania Press, 1987. 96.
4. Ishbel Ross. *Angel of the Battlefield: The Life of Clara Barton.* New York,
NY: Harper & Brothers Publishers, 1956. 45.

Chapter 7. Civil War Heroine

1. Percy H. Epler. *The Life of Clara Barton.* New York, NY: MacMillan
Company, 1917. 67.
2. Ishbel Ross. *Angel of the Battlefield: The Life of Clara Barton.* New York,
NY: Harper & Brothers Publishers, 1956. 51.
3. "Clara Barton at Antietam." *nps.gov.* 25 July 2006. 1 Oct. 2009
<http://www.nps.gov/anti/historyculture/clarabarton.htm>.
4. Ishbel Ross. *Angel of the Battlefield: The Life of Clara Barton.* New York,
NY: Harper & Brothers Publishers, 1956. 51.

Source Notes Continued

Chapter 8. More Work to Be Done
1. Elizabeth Brown Pryor. *Clara Barton: Professional Angel*. Philadelphia, PA: University of Pennsylvania Press, 1987. 134.
2. Stephen B. Oates. *A Woman of Valor: Clara Barton and the Civil War*. New York, NY: Free Press, 1994. 313.
3. Ibid. 381.

Chapter 9. Barton and the Red Cross
1. Percy H. Epler. *The Life of Clara Barton*. New York, NY: MacMillan Company, 1917. 125.
2. Ibid. 144.

Chapter 10. The Red Cross Comes to America
1. Ishbel Ross. *Angel of the Battlefield: The Life of Clara Barton*. New York, NY: Harper & Brothers Publishers, 1956. 130.
2. Elizabeth Brown Pryor. *Clara Barton: Professional Angel*. Philadelphia, PA: University of Pennsylvania Press, 1987. 262.
3. Ishbel Ross. *Angel of the Battlefield: The Life of Clara Barton*. New York, NY: Harper & Brothers Publishers, 1956. 254.
4. Reel 59: General Correspondence, 1838–1912. Clara Barton Papers, Manuscript Division, Library of Congress, Washington, DC.
5. Percy H. Epler. *The Life of Clara Barton*. New York, NY: MacMillan Company, 1917. 433.
6. Ibid. 433.
7. Ishbel Ross. *Angel of the Battlefield: The Life of Clara Barton*. New York, NY: Harper & Brothers Publishers, 1956. 268.
8. "About Us." *American Red Cross*. 5 Apr. 2009. <http://www.redcross.org/portal/site/en/menuitem.d8aaecf214c576bf971e4cfe4 3181aa0/?vgnextoid=477859f392ce8110VgnVCM10000030f3870 aRCRD&vgnextfmt=default>.
9. Percy H. Epler. *The Life of Clara Barton*. New York, NY: MacMillan Company, 1917. xii.

INDEX

Index Continued

ABOUT THE AUTHOR

Susan E. Hamen is a full-time editor who finds her most rewarding career experiences to be writing and editing children's books. Hamen lives in Minnesota with her husband and two young children. In her spare time, she enjoys reading, traveling, and creating memories with her daughter and son. She dedicates this book to her late grandmother, who, like Clara Barton, was a strong, steadfast, and unflappable woman with a kind and generous heart.

PHOTO CREDITS